Plum(b)

poems

Kim Triedman

MAIN STREET RAG PUBLISHING COMPANY
CHARLOTTE, NC

Library of Congress Control Number: 2012953888

ISBN: 978-1-59948-408-2

Produced in the United States of America

Main Street Rag
PO Box 690100
Charlotte, NC 28227
www.MAINSTREETRAG.COM

Acknowledgments:

Selected poems in this collection have been published by the following publications, sometimes in a modified form:

Albatross: "Insurance," "The Day the IUD Came Out"
Myrrh, Mothwing, Smoke: Erotic Poems (Tupelo Press): "Drought," "Siren"
Atticus Review: "Provisions," "Speed," "Wordplay"
The Aurorean: "Think of it This Way:"
bathe in it or sleep (Main Street Rag, 2008): "Best Laid Plans," "Breathless," "Chaos Theory," "Choke-hold," "Distance," "Drought," "Early Thaw," "Fractured," "Gravity," "Harbor," "The Made Bed," "Momentum," "Plagiarism," "Room 402," "Residue"
Blood Lotus: "I Want to be Pablo Neruda—"
Byline Magazine: "Plot," "Momentum"
Clarion Journal: "Plot"
Current Accounts: "Momentum"
Death Hums: "Carrion"
FRiGG Magazine: "The Made Bed"
Ibbetson Street Review: "Accoutrements," "Tell me about middle age"
IF Poetry Magazine: "Socks"
Istanbul Literary Review: "Vines"
The Journal (UK): "Family Portrait," "Room 402"
The Main Street Rag: "Fresh," "The Alchemist"
The New Writer: "Chaos Theory," "Distance," "Fractured"
Poetry International: "Life was easier as a square— "
Poetry Salzburg Review: "Choke-hold"
Poet's Ink: "Drought," "Residue"
Poets for Haiti: An Anthology of Poetry and Art (Yileen Press, 2010): "Life was easier as a square—"

Prairie Schooner: "Plumb," "Unreliable Narrator"
Salamander: "Witch Hazel"
Wilderness House Literary Review: "Bedtime Story,"
    "Plot," "Suffocation"
WomenArts Quarterly: "Signs"

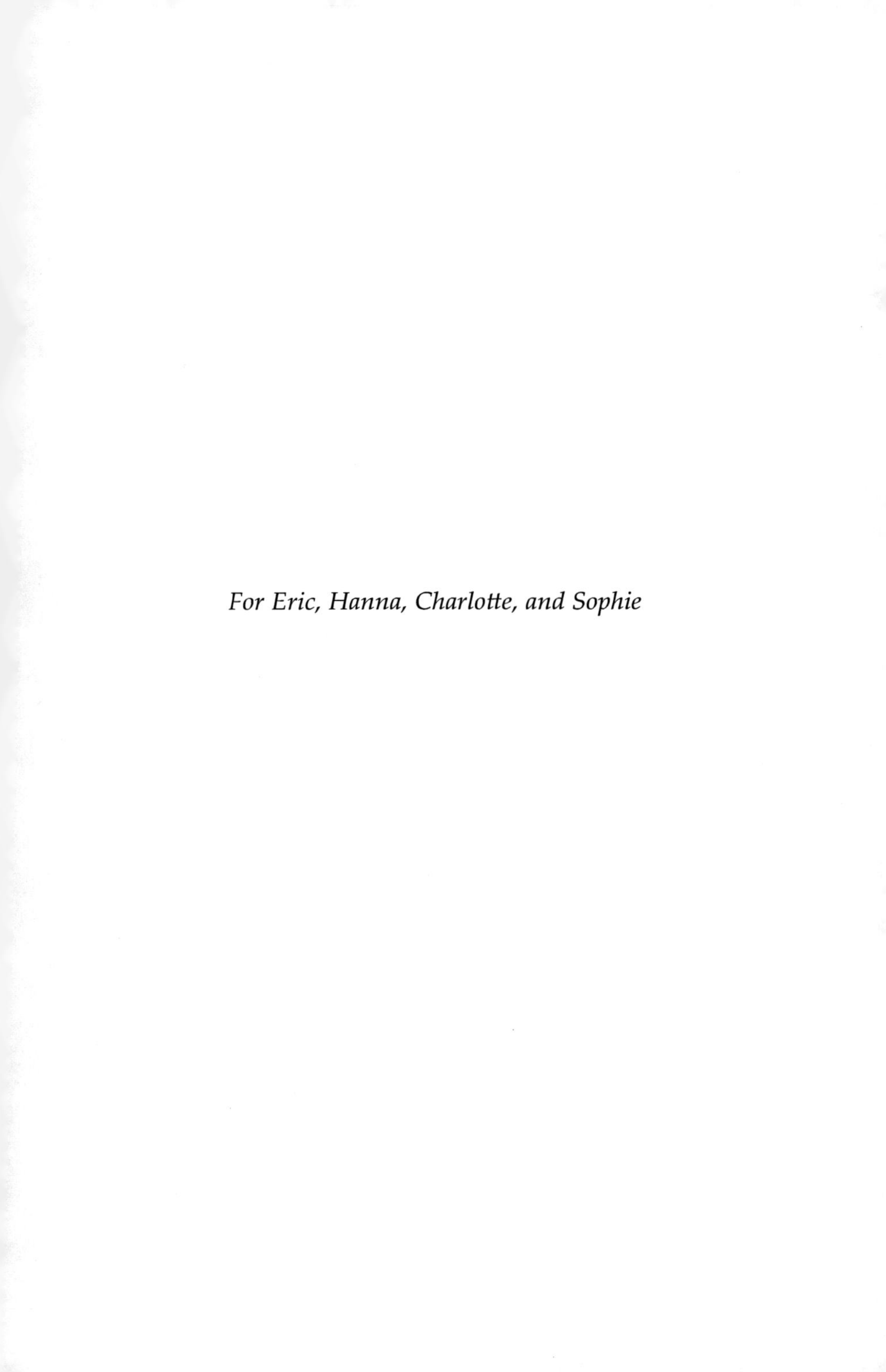

For Eric, Hanna, Charlotte, and Sophie

Contents

Plumb

Plum

Laden

What is a house?

A house is a raincoat.

Is that all?

Walls, minus basements.

Where do you live?

I live. Where.

How do you live?

With the windows open.

PLUMB

WITCH HAZEL

Winters lie long up here—lead-bellied
and mean. Evergreens grow
even darker in the cold.

Outside, the witch hazel
prostrates herself to an unruly wind.

Two people at a small wooden table.
Imagine them taking their morning coffee,
their blue china mugs. A dog
curls beneath them by a cast-iron grate.

Say one of them looks up
and gazes at the sky—absently, perhaps, wondering
about this or that.

An eye
could come to rest upon a small yellow flower—
spindly, unkempt
in its way—
yellow nonetheless. It is

late February—not even the beginning
of the end of winter. New souls
have yet to stir
within the tireless womb.

It is not impossible. Imagine
the flowers came.

Say they even existed.

THINK OF IT THIS WAY:

Between the past and the future
stands a house. It's tidy
and white, nearly ready

to explode. The terror, you see,
the *weight* of such a thing:
neither here nor there, like words

withheld, or the hand
that meant to stroke.
Even in a strong wind leaves

can double-back, and
seagulls hang, frozen
in sky. We sit,

burning in silence,
eyes forward,
remembering nothing.

FRACTURED

Darling

you will

never know. On my way to work the

plane fell from the sky, but just
a small one. The radio played a song
you've never heard before and
my jaw was clamped so tight I couldn't
speak. Everyone thought I was
crazy or just putting on airs; the sheer
humiliation. They said I'd never had
my feet on solid ground. There were no
geese up there, either, they must have sensed
that this was not the best of years
for birds. When I wake these days
my sheets are soaked, the water pools
between my breasts. You sleep like you have
always slept, one foot thrown off
the far end of the bed.

PLUMB

If the walls are made of hair,
imagine then the timbers as bone.

One day we arrived.

We brought with us our money, our
expectations.

We could picture it all

back then —
hearth-hearted, backbone
of stairs, windows opening their eyes
beneath a lintel's earnest brow.

From the gut, we mortgaged
our future.

Time will tell, the basement whispered.
Doors could fly open; gullets
could flare. The grout
could someday seem
a kind of gristle.

*

From here I can tell you

some of the stories.
You see, the way the light,
the way the sun, slantwise, milking
the glass, and the mind
traverses even the oddest
little spaces —

a tiny ravel in the carpet,
the thread-like crack
above the door. There is a nest

of hornets in the wall—
drilling
bumping up
against the plaster. I sit

and wait. Surely
some of them will make it
through—

stingers poised; hindquarters
quivering
with cabined rage.

    *

I slept the deep sleep of a queen.
In my dreams, the walls were plumb;
the windows of the house
were painted black.

If night existed, I could not
see it coming. If there was wind,
there was no evidence—
no disarray, no broken limbs.

Years later, I awoke. The bed was
smaller than it had been. There was
a groaning; the walls began to tremble
and pitch. Through a scratch
in the paint: a gleaming dagger
of moon.

It's nothing, he said. *Go back
to sleep.* He smiled
as he reached for the paintbrush, humming
narcotically.

Beneath the sheet my fingernails
were sickle-black.

*

Each year the wisteria staked its heights
on something larger
than the average house.

It grew and grew.
Once supple, its greenstick fingers
petrified and crooked.

Spring came. The sun warmed
the earth. In summer wood wasps
whined and hurtled through the lacy green.

I did what I did best, sitting
clear-eyed in its dappled shade.

It's no good, he cried. *We'll lose
everything.*

He hacked and hacked.
The wisteria roped her sinewy arms
around the porch.

Never mind, said the fencepost
to the stoop. Between them

a leaf crabbed, the walkway choked
with weeds. Two crows

set down with outspread wings
to juxtapose their shadows.

DROUGHT

The crows, they circle,
dragging their
wretched shadows,
and light tiptoes
gingerly
as day trips into moon
and fields sprawl
in both directions—
bleached; fallow;
studded with want.

Look here,
I am the thirst;
I am the stubble in the field.
Lull me,
I am wanting.
Sink your fingers deep
and fondle my seed.

Coax me.
Wet me.
Color me wheat.

COLOR SCHEME

Evening tipped, spilled
its honey to the earth.

What else was there?
Enough

just to look out the kitchen window,
every morning,
watch each season

displace the one before
like new births, each celebrated
and passed along

in its time
as though nothing ever
really changed. The world

a circle
on the verge of something else—sharper
and more reasonable, with lines
and points and corners around which anything

could be made to happen. She balked
at the threshold, the flagstones in front of her

so perfectly arrayed; jigsaw-
tight. Colors
            staggered

to appear
random in design.

TERRA FIRMA

Forgive me, but I don't know where
to place my foot.

See how the landscape changes, just like that?
The peas, climbing; the corn?
Nothing is where one might expect anymore, reasonably
expect, given all that time and time

before. There are things I know—
eyes, of course, wet wool; the smell of rain
on the tomatoes. Moons
in all their shiny outfits.

But seasons slide beneath our feet
and high above
a hard-billed flicker
taps away
at punky time.

I would go there if I could—
the next place. I would find
a way to breathe.

VINES

Going back would mean
the crisp of frost,
jam jars
lit like jewels
along the window
in the kitchen.
Outside, cows
stomping—
eyes rolled back,
steam-streaming,
tongues thick and damp
as woolen socks.
You make it sound

so easy: the pickets,
the ploughs—
even that fall
we built the sun porch
off the south side
of the house.
You said it was
sturdy, you said
never mind

the trumpet vine—
so breathtaking
each spring—
snaking up silently
beneath the clapboards.

SIGNS

The hostas, for instance,
how leggy they grow
and those rickety ladders
of lusterless blooms. Look, I know

what it is—
an ending again, a sorting out

of times. I can lift my head and see
the contrails
parsing up a church-blue sky,
and the old dog readies herself
for a winter
she may
or may not see.

Beneath the nasturtiums:
dried leaves hang
like crumpled paper hats.

We have been here before, you and I—
a north wind whispers yellow
to the trees, and the old wicker chair sits
waiting, putting on her poker face.

It's only that wayward flock of geese—
recklessly ignoring all the signs—
only they don't seem to know
which way to go.

DISTANCE

Winter coming, and there must be
a score, any score, the whole thing ending
on a cold day, a hard day, each utterance
too complicated to dissect.

There was the glass of wine, too, don't forget that;
there was the overhead light. Cruel,
to be exact. While all around her locusts swarmed
and insults tumbled out of mouths
too tight to form them.

In the refrigerator, a carcass reigned
as though it had something new to offer.

She could hear his voice, faraway as it was.
Between them: cold macadam and dried leaves,
the years flung out like line. She stood,
naked, at the window smeared with grease.
If she knew what he was saying
she didn't let on.

And later, the sheets, pills sliced on the score.
Nighttime dredged of even the tamest of dreams.

LIFE WAS EASIER AS A SQUARE —

razor-edged, an absence
of tilt, corners sharp and sure
as bayonets, pinning it down

to something else.
There was a house
and it was anchored in bedrock,
there was a

plan. Outside the window:
horizons—
gravity—
the steady deployment of seasons
and even a man with a gun,
watching.

Where is he now?

Everything suddenly formless—
edges bleed
and bleed; the chaos
of curve. Even night comes
charging in, and dreams,
unbidden. The mutiny

of seasons.

Above our heads:
blitzkrieg—
gunfire—
rooflines tipping
carelessly toward the sea.

UNSOUND

The foundation sagged in a thousand shades of earth.
The bricks themselves nearly 200 years old,
weathered beyond color to something

akin to wisdom, finer
than just old, layered
with life, everything

giving down to everything else,
silvers to putties to greens, twilight
blues, plum wines, down to the music

of evenings past, autumn fields
and burnished stars, the perfumes
of harvest and battle and love,

even down to the eve
of the first day. A world within a world—
esteemed, entire, gilded

with simple light, if only someone
stopped to notice. How else to see that
the foundation was a fiction, that lives

gave way like rotting timbers on its back.
That far down at the base, down along
the cushioned collar of the earth,

one row of bricks lay powdered to the core,
whiter than white, sifting back down
into the shelter of the soil.

UNRELIABLE NARRATOR

Do you remember the rain, do you remember
the dog barking, didn't she die, wasn't she carried away
in the night with the storm, what time was it then, was it
March, was it spring, was it raining, didn't the water churn
like oceans round our feet, were you there, do you remember
the look on my face, do you remember the rain and the crash
and the dog, barking—

I remember your voice like the trees, even
at night in the wind, I remember the noise, I remember the flashing
of teeth. You wouldn't look me in the eye that night, was it
the time, was it the night, was it the spring, weren't the houses
lit from within and the people in the houses warm and dry,
weren't there clouds, wasn't it raining, what was the dog doing
in the road—

There was the feeling of her weight in my arms
and then only the rain and the smell of spring rain on the dirt, and
there was a moon as the night would have it, yes, of course, do you
remember the moon, do you remember the words, do you remember
you could not look me in the eye, and the rain swallowing our feet
and the promise of more, and the dog in the street, silent,
were you there?—

PLOT

Drawbacks. Cars and kids. Chicken for dinner. Even a Scottish maid
who lost her teeth then moved away. What can I say? My mother
loved me, the beds were high and wide and piled thick with quilts.
Yet still I waken in the night with shaking hands. And winters, too—
they're so much longer than they used to be.

Where do we put it all? Sofas, guilt, the price of gas—all of it
tossed together like so many Sunday casseroles. There is no
orbit here, no perfect round—none of it proceeds as one might expect,
like a novel that circles back to the beginning again, a good novel,
even the tiniest details resurrected; accounted for.

STILL LIFE WITH TIMBER

Empty the pantry of bread, the bottles of wine.
Delete the lines of every song that was sung,
every book that was read. Blow out all of
the candles on all of the cakes for all of
the birthdays. Throw out the baby. Dismantle
the bed.

Never mind—the timbers are still sound
as is the shingling on the roof. The walls
are plumb. In the basement the furnace
still kicks on, throwing off a kind of heat.

CHOKE-HOLD

but winter—
howling,
chill-choked,
knife-blue sky sharpening
its edge against
the iron of the earth.
Every day
an accusation—
branches like bones
pointing,
pewter shards
of ice. It's a lot of

work, this breathing
and breathing:
wind-wheezed,
eyes seamed against
the steel, red hands
weeping white. Air is

less than air.
Even the cypresses
gasping; drained
of color; more black
than green.

SUFFOCATION

At the edge of what one can bear there is a house.
See for yourself. The pickets are white;
they always will be. The path up to the door
is pilfered from the grass. Step inside: there is
no dog. There is a window but the sky is not
admitted by the blinds. I should have known.
The sound you hear is silence. The sound you hear
is your own breathing. Even the walls have learned
to hold their tongues. Mind the sharp corners;
they are everywhere. The dishes shine so hard
they hurt the eyes, and upstairs in the dark
the sheets are starched and neatly folded.
I should have known—the teacups, the spoons.
Once I let myself in the front door. I thought it would
be warm. Once I sat at the table. There was no food.
Once I went upstairs and slipped under the sheets.
They were gone the next day. There is a chill.
Mind the corners. That yawning inside is hunger.
You'd think the air would be so clean.

A FAR CRY

It could be the tundra out there and you could be
far on the other side breaking ice with a pick or trailing
long white scarves of breath behind you as the sun sets
its modest sights on the thin blue line of the horizon.
Along the ice fields time creeps in cold measured inches
the sky fixes its oyster glare and the wind pushes even the farthest
farther away. Think of a train, the silence

left behind. *How cold
is the moon? Did we know this when we lit the first fire?*

FAMILY PORTRAIT

Flames could erupt at any minute
down the hall or
downstairs
in the kitchen a blade
unsheathed
might flash, silver
to blue.
Even in the next room tears
can always spring
unbidden
or hammock themselves
tightly
like corpses
after the blight.

She waits
suspended in the center
quivering
silk peeling from her loins
all eight of her legs
thrumming
to the music of
life's trifling disasters.

RESIDUE

Yesterday there was too much
room in the world. Eyes; breath;
the willow weeping and
always the damage—
words swallowed whole,
tremors at fault lines;
the sharp mean memory of sun,
leaves gone. Still,
occasionally, I find her ballet tights
in the laundry. I fold them slowly,
set them on the stair up to her room.
On the phone she sounds
quite breathless—a paper's due;
the Kirov's coming to New York
next month. She speaks so fast
I only listen to the speed.

It's obvious now: time
rushing through and standing still;
the sky, aubergine.
None of it planned—
not the wind circling like hawks,
not the blight. It's dark at four,
her shins are tired; I wonder is it
late enough to pour a glass of wine?
The house fills up with too much space,
each cat now has a room
to call her own. I used to love
my bedroom door, but now
I leave it open.

Between breaths, the only lasting solace
the table—the lamp—the thick round
custard of light.

VERMIN —

in the walls now,
by the corner of the bed,

thumping and tumbling, wheeling
in vertical circles,
gouging at the insides
of the house.

He cannot sleep.

Lying in bed at night he suffers
their insurrection—every scrape
of every claw.

I close my eyes, smile
to myself. Picture them
cavorting. Dream them into
wantonness sublime.

MURDER

It is lovely. The bleeding heart
has come and gone.

Here, in the garden, the pulse
quickens, eyes and hands quiver
over lupine and thrift.

She surveys the flowers,

ruthlessly, wielding
sharp things, decides coolly
between fuschias and blues

as though some small life
depended on it,
her own

tenuous shoots weakened,
besieged on all sides by
loosestrife
and snakeroot,
the strange, strangling incursion

of mint.

Even that primrose over there—
her carpet of chromium
goodwill—they smile at each other
with blood-lusty eyes.

PLUM

THE SLAUGHTERHOUSE

It was a mad scene at the poultry store.
Live Chickens Fresh Killed!
The Portuguese part of town—
down on its heels but lively, too—
plump women and flashes of red.
The line was

out the door. I was in love,
of course; there was nothing
I could do. I could have found
precious in a lump of coal.

FRESH

Leave September to its own devices
and what do you expect?

Even along the ocean you can smell
the concord grapes, even with an off-shore breeze,
even when all you're looking for is
some clarity and peace

of mind, and this morning at the market
the pomegranates were on fire, burning
with lust or shame, I'm not sure
which. All I wanted was

an apple to bite into, juicy
but firm, something to revive me mid-morning
with a second cup of coffee

but it was Whole Foods, of course,
and the apples were confusing
and the produce man was

surprisingly attractive
and the passion fruit was displayed
prominently
right there by the sliding doors.

FLESH

The fall—
cherries cleaving, apples gleaming
seductively on their stems.
Leaves gyrate and blush, light filters
through the deepening branches.
Every act reverberates, even those evenings
not too long ago, that tiny nuanced smile,
there's something so long and irreducible about all of it,
something so—

Tell me I'm wrong, but doesn't it
change everything—*the past? the rest?*—
doesn't the one small thing
elaborate
like nerves
into a thousand other things?
Doesn't something grow, like fruit, but wrongheaded?
Imagine yourself

in the bite of an apple—
the snap,
the sweet,
the rivered juice. Let seeds fall

SPEED

Looking back there were no secrets, only life
careening on its side, reckless
and innocent, dragging with it
the grass and the gravel, the infant
trees along the embankment. She was

there, saw the birds scatter, felt the burn
of rubber like a deep black inhalation. The sky

waited, empty
and flat, but in the kitchen a refrigerator hummed
its disapproval and overhead the lights hissed
blue, blue
as though it even mattered. Everyone already

knew. It was in the tarnish, the grit,
those great billowing clouds
of dissimulation. It spurted and choked, unspooled
in the rear-view —

Her choice of car.
The shifting of gears.
A heedless destination.

BIRTH

Ours began barefoot, as things should.

Cries were uttered —
life howling through gaping holes
and arms and legs shuddered
lightning-shocked. Eyelids parted
to admit only as much light
as eyes could bear.

After the frenzy — quiet,
light lightly, breath; bodies
gone slack and heads rolled back
to reveal not even the trace
of a smile. Only

the wonder —

the wonder —

the perfect hollow round
of disbelief.

DOMESTIC DISTURBANCE

Suffer the wind—the chimes
on the dogwood

ever more frantic
and the flag across the street

persevering, capitulating,
working ever harder

to conceal its exhaustion.
Say it keeps coming

and coming and the house moans
in protest and the dog

takes to sleeping with one eye open
and even at night there is

the slick of black leaves
sticking to the windows

and the hurl of old-growth trees
tossing their heavy heads

against the sky.
Say you pull

the shades.
Say you lie

alone reading under
thick, woolen blankets, swaddled

and safe. Your book
is long. Your eyes stay

fastened to the page.
Even here a sharp gust

rattles the old storms,
and you feel a quickening

deep
in your deep middle,

whether or not
you desire it.

THUNDERHEADS RISING

Mineral tang, heat puddling the boulevard.
Small peeps of nuthatches against a fast wall
of silence. Even with her eyes closed, she can
feel it—nerve-surge, skin slick-glisten then prick
with whispered cool, the heat of the day still holding
it's stale breath. Overhead the Norway maples wait

for the turn, hurl their furling leaves, ready themselves
for the curtain of rain.

HARBOR

The wind a ruthless thing,
feral. Branches shredding
a paper-white sky.

Imagine the house, the light
in the window —
honeyed, pulpy, weeping
like a womb.

I am there, if you like:
I am the woman in the
broth. Stir me,
I will feel it. Take me
to your mouth. Imagine me
over and over again —

suet, camphor, balm.

DINNER AT TRYST

Let me put on my glasses so I may
savor you: citrus-spray of lines
around the mouth, slow eyes of dough
rising. Even your hands—the sinew,
the flesh, curing, the way they wait
and wait—the butter of your sudden smile.

Let me muddle the soft mint of you;
sup of your custard—the eggs,
the milk.

THE MADE BED

Before you, there was the knowledge—
warm, taut, breath reversed;

imprint preceding hand
dampness anticipating kiss—

only a shape, back then, a space

between words
between skin.

Something would come, I knew,
a color perhaps—blood

orange, something
like flame. The bed
was waiting—

white sheets clean and
softened with age, pillows
smoothed
silent
plumped.

ROOM 402

Starting here the ground goes soft
and Chinese lanterns dance on their wires,
spilling blood at the feet of good people.
Rules are broken and contracts are broken,
assumptions dropped from mean heights
like melons; the soft fuzzed heads
of newborn girls. All that was, was—
days like hedgerows; nights curled tight
inside themselves like rage, sliding snake-like
on dry bellies to this strange unholy place.

Starting here, babies are grown men
and grown men are angry; frozen; gruesome
to behold—like death back-loaded, or
the opposite of womb—and anger
starting here is loud and fetid and
full of teeth and what we do with it has
everything to do with the softness of the ground,
the softness,
the lanterns,
the waning of the moon,
the tiny but insistent voice
of the color of flame.

BEDTIME STORY

Tell me again —

a world within a world,
greening in winter, bursting,
cleaving like warm fruits.
Even when the winds howled,
even then, there was a fire
in the middle, banked
and blue, there were
simple burnished stars
like embers in the sky. If only
your hand—if only
the time it found its way up to my lips—

tell me again
how that story ends.

SIREN

She has a pillbox, he said,
but hair like flame
spills down her back. Otherwise
there was a hatchet in her car, and
next: that ruby patch
of poison ivy. It was

too much, he said — her hair
spills down her back,
words fall from her like bits
of burning ash. At midday just

a windless calm.
Somewhere out there
he hears the wail of a siren,
and he steps outside,
barefoot,
without thinking.

SOCKS

I've often fancied you with just socks and a briefcase—
black socks, that is, and maybe it's strange but no stranger
really than anything else, than the light in the room
for example or the dog. *Details* is what I mean to say
plus you never looked half-bad, either, even from behind.
It's just a snapshot, just like any other—not a world, not a
war—just a moment, the kind that maybe sticks around for awhile
or not but it does that thing, anyhow: the way the muscle
it twitches—eyes, lips, heart—light tripping on and off
like a loose bulb in an old socket, the way for just a moment
you breathe and you breathe and you recognize
with a clean and ancient joy

that you are breathing.

BREATHLESS

I have counted
the buttons on your shirt
and released them,
every one—
stared silent and stung
as the fields of you
unfold before me.
I have sunk my hands deep
into your earth,
pressed it in my fists,
held it up to my face
to breathe. I have touched it
with my tongue.

Bury me now.
Fill my throat to choking.
Bespread my body.
Press down on me
like swollen loam:
fecund, full.

EARLY THAW

The geese were flying west today; it was the
last straw. Crocuses penetrating,
underwear off before noontime; breath held
thin and high above the collarbone.
I should have guessed: the groping
and the mouthing—endlessly—the dampness
of the earth. Important, *exuberant*—
life asserting itself, insistent
as tongue. Bosoms, hips, the stark white canvas
of throat. Outside the window—
puddles of snowmelt. Birdsong. Cats splaying
shamelessly in the sun on the front walk.

PLAGIARISM

after Tony Hoagland

Hey babe.
I have a wonderful poem for you

but it's someone else's.
Something about stains and time
and the color of sky—beauty, of course;
relentless. That

phrase he used—
        the very tint of inexperience—
it made me want to
bathe in it or sleep; break silently
at a very unlikely angle. The world is

capable of such things—drowning us
on a whim. There are
winter shadows, thin as wire,
and the sky outside my window is
breathless with blue. Above the chimney:
earnest plugs of smoke.
You are that

stain, of course, the one
I can't get out—

ruinous
glorious
immutable.

LOST IN TRANSLATION

I thought you said *yes*
or something like it, something
juiced, a plum, and time out there
calling and calling, moons swaddling us
like silvered gauze. I thought there were
eyes talking, mouths hearing every
single word, not to mention the pulse.

But enough about you.

Perhaps you didn't know
that when I tip my head the clouds
no longer matter, nor the light;
that the red fruits on the dogwood
fall without a sound. Even that
thing we made—glitter and fire
and silk—that thing we never really knew
how to hold,

I have lost that, too.

OLD-GROWTH

Ignore the rain. Leave the maple
to her own devices, crook-fingered and stripped

of everything that ever mattered.
The grasses at her feet are long; they ride
the dips and mounds of hardened earth
like thinning hair, straw-white
and slack. It was

like this: I used to wear
your socks. Radiators played their flutes
above the night, the sound alone
enough to keep us warm.
In one strange act I brought you
paper-whites and wine, three perfect plums
just to see you juggle.

But all the while she stood
her ground, dressing and undressing,
marking the tiresome moods
of the sun, skin knobbed now with age,
arthritic arms—even
in winter—sleeved in moss.

LATE HARVEST

Pick the pears along the way.
It is late. I can feel the earth
slip and sometimes I bare
the pale moon of my breast
to the sky. I am inclined

not to worry. The trees have done
what trees will do—
grown up around us,
hidden us in shadow,
shuddered
in the deep paroxysm of night

and gone still.

LADEN

CHAOS THEORY

Come this way.
The tree out my window is bare now
then full of leaves; many things, actually, and
the sky likewise changes. Just now there is
the threat of white.

Sometimes: no birds.

I have been here—forever, really—
watching, waiting with a thirst. It may
not seem like much but you will see:
the stories are like the light,
so when I crane my neck a little to the left
the sun is either bleeding or it's not.
Today the road is veined with salt,
but once a moon stared back at me,
blank and unforgiving.

Sometimes there are tears, but there are
copper pennies, too, and glasses of milk;
mothers with no teeth. Paths
abound: citrine, the smell of limes,
kudzu dark and pulpy and heavy as loss.
I have seen a Muslim woman walking
in the wind, her burkha like a flying shroud,
and then the sky above her head
go black with beating birds.

Come this way. I will try to protect you.
I have watched men starve along the way,
half lost, and then devour themselves
like serpents. You will see.
The light this way may be too harsh;
the noise of endless wars. Colors—
mutinous. There are no walls, only space
and then more space—timeless;
perpetual.

Even on a bad day I will feel you
breathe. It may be quiet. It may be
quiet; only limes.

Come this way.

MILK

Begin at the beginning.
There is the breast.
There is the memory of womb.

The world has its own thoughts on these things.
It becomes unreliable.
Sometimes there is cheese for lunch;
sometimes—no cheese.
Who can say why?
One day we're taught to hold our tongues;
the next we're told to speak
what's on our mind.

You grow, you grab
onto whatever you can—a slogan,
a sophomore, a shtick.
Lifestyles emerge, and children
and children. The house is
spanking clean. Even the milk—
gleaming; pasteurized.

The rooms are empty now—
only the knowledge, like a hole.
The only breasts you know
are yours—empty too.

MOMENTUM

On the fifth day of the snow
the daughter leaves, saying,
I may be back.
The sky does not exist.
In the kitchen: soup, simmering
until the end of time.

The mother.
It is the long hour before dinner,
and dark. She walks,
from the kitchen to the hallway
and turns, looks back
to the beginning.

On the fifth day of the snow
the daughter leaves, saying
I have no choice.
The sky exists, but elsewhere
and oh so many colors. There is
a pulse, like drums, there is
the suckling red.

No, she says, gathering her
things about her, *I don't care
for any soup.*

INSURANCE

There is one thing I get right: every spring I plant
the nasturtiums. My husband shakes his head,
says: *For god's sake, why don't you just do
pansies like everyone else?* I know better. It's
insurance, I say. He walks off and shrugs, turns on
his weed whacker. I go about my business, not
planting pansies, stuffing fat seeds into thin holes
punched too close together: packing the future tight.
It's a long summer but a short one, too—
iris to coreopsis to New England aster, suns up and
down. Come September the evenings grow chill.
Kids are off, the house goes mute, dried oak leaves
scritch along the walk like small, arthritic hands.
Only the nasturtiums are becoming: teeming—
cascading—extrapolating—luxuriating in their
greenness, even the blossoms, tipped in gold, their
little open mouths…

TELL ME ABOUT MIDDLE AGE.

What is there to know?
The bottom sags. Milk runs
from the eyes. You look outside and
what you see

is fall. Even in spring, even in summer,
the trees have a way of
prefiguring chill. And when
the sun is warm you feel
both its presence

and its absence. Lives can
snap—cleanly—or just
lurch along from day to day
like crabbed leaves in the wind.
And always the children—coming,

going—each one
like ballast in your chest.
Even the sweetest autumn fruit—
the apples, the pears,
the clustered purple grapes—
they weigh so heavy
in your hands.

STILL LIFE WITH FRUIT

Don't forget the chickens; hands sunk
in a pillow of dough.

There was the barn, there was
the souring hay; fields out back stripped
and turned and tinder-dry.

Evenings you could smell
the burning pile, the rotting fruit.
In the rose garden a bronze sundial
perched silently on its pedestal,
marking off the hours,
as though time itself could be
counted
or weighed
or held neatly in the palm of one hand.

Something was about to end.

PINK LADY

Fitting, perhaps—these fruits
just beginning to turn.

I am laden.

Looking down I see
the childhoods—

dappled; apple
cheek'd.

I am the bearer, the witness

tree—
sheltering,
rooted,
unable to leave.

BEST LAID PLANS

This is how it works:

You are there—
the slap, the squall. You make the
breakfasts, such as they are, the beds;
feel the foreheads with your lips.

Winter boots. Suns, up and down. They cry or they
laugh; eventually, they grow
breasts.

Sometimes, a difficult night.

This, too, is how it works:

You stay put.
The years slide beneath your feet.

You are here, they are there, them with their breasts,
their apartments. You still with your
lips. They are breathless; there will be
Thanksgivings and
Futures. Their tears, when they come, are pressed
flat against their palms.

This is how it works:

You—
still with your lips

THE DAY THE IUD CAME OUT

You don't need it anymore, he said.

It had been 18 years, the suddenness
like a slap.

My youngest was off to St. Louis in the fall.
I said, *I wish she could have stayed
a little closer to home.* But he was

distracted —
forceps, a tug and a gasp, that quick sharp
in-draught of air.

It was done before I caught my breath.

For a heartbeat he held the bloodied
T-square in his hand. Peeling off his gloves
he drew it deep into the latex shroud;
tossed it like a condom in the bin.

Just a little staining today.

POEM

Arrive for me fully formed—
tearing at membranes, fatted
and fleshed, still sluiced
with the vernix of creation.
Let each toe be tallied
to a perfect ten, each finger
curled with the precision
of a fisted bud. I have known it—
sturm und drang, the slipping
of film into form. Come—
come to me now. Lay yourself
down on my white blanket
in your bloodied, brilliant, god-
awful mess.

GRAVITY

It's all about the uterus, anyway—
brown rooted things and marl, buds
like new nipples; the twining of vetch.
Give me something to go by—
ropey and rich—give me
menstrual blood. There is a kind
of peace.

CARRION

I have seen the vultures with their glutton-eyes.
The poets, too,

circling, peering down a blank
and silent sky. Something

will happen; the sun will drag
its bloodied corpse
towards the night. And carcasses, too—

entrails heaped
like gifts across the road.
Sure, there will be

dying. So much
good meat.

WORDPLAY

It's come to this, has it? Scouring the paper
for clues, anything
flammable, kindling for the furnace
in the basement of the house
so newly empty?

A child. Likewise, other things:
fences, potted plants, your mother's
breakfront like an anchor—equally
complicit.

Words came easily, filled in
for all the cracks. When the wind blew
only the quietest among us could tell
that anything was wrong.

Now, silence. In the morning,
I cut phrases from the paper—

a grim anniversary

    still wary of bonds

They litter the un-swept floor.

When I reach for the kettle, the house
rises up as if to mock the ground
it stood on.

I WANT TO BE PABLO NERUDA—

the tongue of my mind slipping
over fishheads, pyres burning blue
and loose-limbed men pressing into
soft things the color of pie. I want
the death-word to have a capital D;
bodies swollen and purpled with sex;
thin boys with sharp knives.
I want gargoyles and flatware,
flesh slick and deep as murky ponds,
and I want the shiver that follows,
lightly.

I know—wish hard enough and
walls come down: skies weep,
birds bleat out nasty songs,
and leaves turn like wayward children,
brown to green. There's an itch on my back,
way up where I can't scratch it;
I want something he has—a cure,
glittered— I want his twelve-inch wand.
I want the star at the top to be
rusted and barbed, sharp enough
to draw black blood.

THE ALCHEMIST

The good doctor
came into my house, a perfect

stranger,
armed with his bag full

of dying. In the middle of the kitchen rug—
the dog, prostrate, stranded finally

in her old age
on an island of red braid.

He spoke to her and held
her gaze, sitting down there with

the breathing and the beating,
opening

his bag, hiding
nothing, embracing

something needle-fine
yet vast, too:

the dog and me and her death
all as one thing, one

perfect thing we might just
give to one another, an alchemy

of living
and of dying.

This stranger. This perfect
conjurer. This island home.

THE MAGICIAN

And grief begat grief, he said,
and the dog died
a good death but the emptiness
would not lie still.
See here, I have

nothing in my hands—
children grown or never born, a lover scarcely
touched. Even the mother, coughing,
counting out the ragged breaths.

Look at my sleeve, these colored scarves,
they just keep coming

and coming—

tug to tug,
blue
to red
to green.

MOVE OVER

The girl in the story is old now and short of breath—

The girl—

The girl in the story is old now, just look at her neck the
backs of her hands just smell that sour-belly breath—

The girl—

In the story the girl looks at her old-lady neck breathes into
her hands and smells—

The girl smells—

On her hands the girl smells the cold cream her mother
once used on her—

Like her mother the girl smoothes the cold cream in slow-
motion circles—

Slow-motion—

Circles of shadow under her eyes, and when she coughs
tiny sprays of lines around her—

The girl coughs, smoothes the lines around her mouth
where the dimples once were—

So smooth, her granddaughter says, feeling the soft-warm
dough of her upper arm—

On the sofa, the girl—the granddaughter—says—

The girl says—

The girl says, *how old are*

SURVIVAL

After so many miles logged and the days
still come up rosy or gristle with the heavy hand
of a god bent on heavier things and with no more
than the false bottom of the lies we tell ourselves
and the prayers we mouth to shore up the lies the dog
still sits with her paws lightly crossed,
perfect as pie. Never mind

the abundance of flowers, that was just
a game I played one spring day trying to make it *so*
and *so*
and filling the space with so much color it had to be
good it had to be

comprehensive in the way of carpeting
or anesthesia and all the while the sun spilled
its golden trinkets through the branches as though
someone intended the world to break
your heart, the wine, too,
soothing, swaddling, enunciating the word *Beauty*
in a kind of sermon or stand-up act meant for those who
might be
made to believe, but I know the mosquitoes
still come out on cue, chasing down the light
like sparrows in pursuit, the lone hawk
its yellow eyes roving steadily coolly purposefully
across the humming ground.

ACCOUTREMENTS

I have learned.
This winter when I re-painted the living room
I checked in with the others first. *Yellow*
was the consensus—not a color
I would have chosen.

Pale, they said, *like straw*, they said.
Muted, discrete.

Thus recognized, they went back to things
unrelated to color.

But I smiled on my way to the paint store.
I knew that there was still
a universe out there—
the yellows of emperors and cowards;
the yellow of bile.

When the room was finished, everyone
was delighted. *Yes, of course,*
they cooed, *it was the perfect choice
of color.* No one seemed even
to notice the lesser of my domestic
gambits—

A *trompe l'oeil* hearth.
Sheer lace for the windows.
The blood-orange of the new settee.

PROVISIONS

I bought one pomegranate this morning just to admire it.
They were two for five dollars, but I was only
purchasing color.

Can we eat it? my daughter asked that evening.
She was limping through her chemistry homework,
watching me watching the pomegranate.

Not until I'm finished, I answered vaguely,
wondering what exactly that meant.

It sat on the counter, defining red. Even the tomatoes
knew not to argue.

When my husband came home, he palmed it absently
then rolled it down the hallway for the dog.

It's in my office, now, catching the afternoon sun.
I'm not sure why it matters so much
but it does. I know that the seeds inside are
waiting, jewel-like, encrusted in their pulpy womb.
But for the moment I'm content just to
see it there when I turn my head. Sitting
quietly on the sill. Concentrating all that color
in one place.

With Gratitude

To my family, in its sprawling iterations, with special thanks to my mom for the exquisite artwork.

To Joanne DeSimone Reynolds, Donna Johnson, Matthew Rose, and Paul Simeone, ongoing and forever.

To my various poetry groups, ever-changing but certainly including Jo, Lorian, Laura, Ariadne, Ann, Diane, Joan, Donna, Melissa, Mary, Sheryl, Betsy, Sara, Alice, Martha, Chris, and my various comrades at Colrain.

To Nadia Herman Colburn, Wendy Mnookin, Tom Daley, Joan Houlihan, and Jeffrey Levine, mentors all. To Fred Marchant, goodest guy. To Michael Meyerhofer. And to the all-embracing Bards of the Au Bon Pain…